QUILT VISIONS

2004

CELEBRATING THE ART OF THE QUILT

An Exhibition of Forty-Five Quilts

Edited by Patti Sevier

QUILT SAN DIEGO / QUILT VISIONS

Acknowledgements

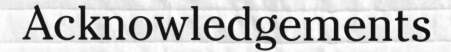

It is the collective vision of many individuals that has made this, the eighth biennial juried international exhibition of Quilt San Diego/Quilt Visions possible. I would like to extend my gratitude and appreciation to the following individuals:

Members of the Board of Directors of Quilt San Diego/Quilt Visions:
Phyllis Newton, Miriam Machell, Kathleen McCabe, Margrette Carr, Kay Lettington, Suzanne MacGuineas, Phyllis Morrow, and Susan Swisher.

Jurors for **Quilt Visions 2004**: Liz Axford, Michael Monroe, Jane Sauer
Photographer: Mike Campos of Campos Photography
Technical Assistance: Ben Sevier

We are grateful to our partners in the production of this exhibit, the beautiful Oceanside Museum of Art. The following individuals at OMA have provided invaluable assistance during all phases of the production of **QUILT VISIONS 2004**: James R. Pahl, Beth Smith and especially Peggy Jacobs.

Copy editing: Margrette Carr, Barbara Friedman, Tina Rathbone

Patti Sevier
President, Board of Directors
Quilt San Diego/Quilt Visions

A Visions Publication
PMB# 372
12463 Rancho Bernardo Road
San Diego, CA 92128-2143

Cover Art - *Northern Light* by Leesa Zarinelli Gawlik

Library of Congress Cataloging-in-Publication Data
LC # 2004097056
ISBN - 09724664-1-X

Printed in Hong Kong through Global Interprint.

Oceanside Museum of Art

Oceanside Museum of Art is pleased to present **Quilt Visions 2004**. Throughout its ten-year history of exhibitions and public programs the museum has established a reputation as a center for contemporary textile art. That distinction was strengthened in 2002 when the international quilt exhibitions of Quilt San Diego/Quilt Visions were incorporated into the museum's exhibition cycle. Submissions from around the world were viewed by a distinguished panel of jurors who selected the works for this spectacular biennial event. This year, 45 art quilts were chosen from 607 works sent by artists in 15 countries. The result is an extraordinary survey of contemporary art quilts, replete with the breathtaking passion, design, and craftsmanship that one would expect to find in a vibrant art form that is flourishing today.

Many individuals have generously given their time, energy and expertise to make this project possible. Patti Sevier, Quilt San Diego President, and Treasurer Miriam Machell have once again organized a highly professional production. I wish to thank them and the other members of the QSD board for their dedication and commitment to this elegant art form. Special thanks also go to jurors Liz Axford, Michael W. Monroe and Jane Sauer for accepting the formidable task of selecting the work in this exhibition from the many exceptional pieces submitted.

Visitors will be richly rewarded for spending time with the museum's welcoming and knowledgeable docents. I wish to thank Docent Director Ginny Tompkins and her carefully trained OMA Docents for their commitment to the educational mission of the museum and for so capably guiding visiting groups through the exhibition. Thanks also go to Kay Lettington, Phyllis Newton, and the Quilt San Diego/Quilt Visions docents for graciously providing daily docent services for individual visitors and unscheduled groups.

Lastly, special thanks to Peggy Jacobs, Chair of OMA's Exhibitions Department for her handsome exhibition design and for the excellent coordination of this grand project.

James R. Pahl
Executive Director

Jurying Philosophy

*W*e define a work of art as a work that is in some way extraordinary. It is expressive and invites us to see ourselves and the world anew, or inspires us in a new way.

*W*e want the best in quiltmaking today. It is certainly not our intention to shock the public. While it is important to represent the range of today's quiltmaking, it is equally important that each quilt possess a vitality of its own and be able to stand alone as well as work with the other quilts to provide an exhibition that somehow "gels" together.

*W*e want the public to see a range of quilts, some that perhaps may initially "feel" familiar and also those that will make them stop and think, evoke an emotion, create an opinion. We want quilts that derive from the necessity to communicate, that speak from the soul of the quiltmaker.

*W*e want quilts that flow with color, sparkle with excitement, those that make visual impact, and those that are so subtle that one must look closely to see unusual use of fabric, high technical skills, and other marvelous effects used to create the design.

*W*e want all those wonderful, incredible quilts that express the quiltmaker's creativity. We want an exhibition that compels the viewer to return for more than one look.

Liz Axford

Liz Axford is a quiltmaker and surface designer who lives and works in Houston, Texas. Her work has been included in many juried shows including Quilt National, Crafts National, Fiberarts International and Materials: Hard and Soft. She was the 1998 recipient of the Quilt Visions Quilt Japan Prize, and in 2001 was chosen to be one of five inaugural Resident Artists at the newly formed Houston Center for Contemporary Craft.

Thank you to the dedicated and highly-organized Quilt Visions volunteers who, by making our job logistically simple, allowed us to concentrate on the difficult task of selecting the work. The staff and volunteers of the Oceanside Museum of Art made us feel at home in their town. Exhibition Coordinator Peggy Jacobs' preliminary layout of the show as we approached our final decisions enabled us to choose the maximum number of pieces that could be comfortably displayed in the small, elegantly proportioned space.

Just as submitting slides to a juried exhibit is a serious undertaking, and not for the faint of heart, jurying the work of one's peers is a difficult task and a serious responsibility. Quilt Visions' Jurying Philosophy stated that we were to choose a show of quilts that are "somehow extraordinary," that "speak from the soul of the quiltmaker," that possess "high technical skills."

What did that mean for me? It meant quilts that communicated something personal about the artist and his or her concerns; command of the chosen techniques was a given. When the artist submitted multiple entries, I wanted there to be a connection between them – a thread of definitive style and/or content – something that made the body of work viewed greater than the sum of the parts. I wanted to see quilts at least somewhat different from anything I'd seen before, yet equally connected to the history of quiltmaking.

Quilts that particularly resonated with me were often of simple composition, with strong visual and/or emotional impact. In Nancy Cordry's *Cacti 1,* bits of color dance across the surface; Ruth Garrison's *Net 4* is bold and self-confident in its use of pure color. Conversely, Pamela Fitzsimon's *Fossil Bed #3* is all about subtlety - the slight sheen of the stained silk; the hand quilting pulled up just tight enough to create a lovely puckered surface. Bean Gilsdorf's *Frequency* hints at a dark narrative, but the viewer is left to piece together the story; in Lori Lupe Pelish's *Bad News,* we've stumbled into a difficult moment in this family's life – will it be shared with us? Mi Sik Kim's *The Wall* and Emily Richardson's *Before a Gate* invite us to walk into the worlds they create, to engage with every part of them.

It was exciting to see so many dynamic and sometimes provocative works in slide form, whether or not they became a part of the final selection. I am grateful for the enormous difficulty of our decisions. I look forward to viewing the show in person, when the low relief of the quilting adds an entirely new dimension, bringing the work fully alive.

Jane Sauer

Jane Sauer is Artistic Director of Thirteen Moons Gallery, Santa Fe, New Mexico. A curator, studio artist, lecturer, juror, recipient of two National Endowment for the Arts Grants, member of the American Craft Council College of Fellows, and past Chair of the American Craft Council, she has exhibited nationally and internationally, including in the Biennale Internationale de la Tapisserie Lausanne.

I want to take this opportunity to commend the members of Quilt San Diego/Quilt Visions and the staff of the Oceanside Museum of Art for the professional and meticulously organized jury process. The presentation of slides, independence allowed the jurors, and immediate space analysis made this experience intellectually rich and impressively fair to each person who entered. All three jurors, Liz Axford, Michael Monroe and I worked diligently to create a cohesive exhibition of the full range of contemporary quiltmaking.

The first viewing of slides presented the jurors with an overview of everything submitted. The next round eliminated almost half of the slides. Sadly for the jurors, who desired to give each applicant a chance to have their work thoroughly judged, we had to eliminate a number of entries because of the poor quality of the slide. As always, the question arose "Did the artist ever project the slide before sending it to represent their work?" The artist should keep in mind that the image seen on the screen is the only link to the eye and mind of the juror.

As the rounds of viewing, discussion, and scoring progressed, more eliminations were made. The jurors looked for a consistent body of work by an artist even though only one piece could be selected for final exhibition. An artist with only one submission looked weaker than one with three submissions. An artist with work demonstrating three different directions appeared to be less mature than an artist who had found a personal voice. As the rounds progressed and it was clear that we still had too many quilts for the space, we discussed, debated, negotiated and compromised with each other. The final round took longer than several of the earlier rounds together and miraculously we agreed on an exhibit.

Our final choices represent an exciting array of diverse and extraordinary art quilts. We selected quilts that reflect the influence of the history of quilting and that convey personal imagery derived from the artist's hand, imagery that goes beyond the allure of technique. Personal diary, choice of materials, layers, chemical effects, geometry, and improvisations reflect the ways in which artists who construct quilts are deeply engaged in the physical act of constructing imagery, pattern, abstraction, figurative or landscape, that is closer to the edge and transcending the expected.

Michael W. Monroe

Michael Monroe has been involved with contemporary American craft for over 30 years. Prior to his current role as an independent curator, writer and advisor, Monroe served as executive director of the American Craft Council, and as Past President of the Peter Joseph Gallery in New York City. For 21 years, Monroe was associated with the Smithsonian American Art Museum's Renwick Gallery. The museum collects and presents exhibitions featuring the creative achievements of craft artists and designers in the United States. From 1974, two years after the museum opened, Monroe served as Curator until 1986 when he became Curator-in-Charge, a position he held until 1995. From 1971 to 1974, Monroe directed the Fine Arts Gallery and taught design for the State University of New York, Oneonta.

It was an honor to have been invited to serve as one of three jurors for **Quilt Visions 2004**. The formidable jurying task was made all the more pleasurable due to the well articulated charge we received from the passionate members of the board of directors of Quilt San Diego/Quilt Visions . They stressed the importance of "selecting the finest examples from among the numerous submissions, those quilted pieces that would validate and promote quiltmaking as a true art form."

With these challenging words in mind we set off on an unparalleled visual and cerebral journey through the rich and varied possibilities as seen through the eyes of artists, both here and abroad. The global community of quilters is represented in this final selection with excellent examples of nearly every genre of imagery including minimalism, geometric formalism, abstract expressionism, realism, pop, narration, humor, portraiture, social commentary, and landscape. Today's quilter continues to explore the rich possibilities of techniques and various styles by masterfully manipulating the elements of art to achieve a clarity and unity of expression.

My personal criteria for making informed decisions can be summed up in the following thoughts: For me, the strongest quilts pursue an original idea while interpreting older traditions and /or techniques in a fresh way. Their makers most often find inventive solutions to design problems instead of repeating trite or contrived ones. They also evidence a masterful handling of materials and techniques, not as ends in themselves, but rather in the service of their ideas. The strongest artists understand materials and their inherent possibilities and limitations, but above all they recognize a material's appropriateness for use in their quilted creation. Additionally I embrace those quilts that embody a strong and vital connection between the maker's idea and the final expression of his or her idea. For these makers, no "disconnects" exist between idea and execution. For artists who submitted more than one quilt I felt it was important to have each one share common underlying themes and techniques as opposed to presenting distinctly different works lacking in cohesion of thought and execution. Finally, my most important criterion is to be sure that each quilt communicates to the viewer a sense of feeling and caring on the part of the maker. The final selection of quilts announce themselves as objects of personal expression; they resound with the artist's confidence, verve, imagination, and inventiveness. For them, we are grateful.

It is hoped that this exhibition will highlight and call attention to the significant contributions made by quilters to contemporary visual art, and inspire an awareness of these extraordinary artists. As the 21st century opens, the most technologically advanced of our history, these quilts stand as testimony to a belief in the value of works of the mind, eye, and hand. Despite our increasing reliance on computers, the intimate and physical qualities of handmade quilts have never had more appeal.

Sponsors

Quilt San Diego/Quilt Visions recognizes the many wonderful individuals and organizations that have so generously given of their time and financial resources to make this exhibition possible.

ROSIE GONZALEZ
Rosie's Calico Cupboard

We would like to acknowledge Rosie Gonzalez, owner of Rosie's Calico Cupboard Quilt Shop, as a benefactor and true friend to this exhibition. We are especially grateful for her unfailing support during the last ten years.

Bali Fabrics

El Camino Quilters

E. E. Schenck Company

Glendale Quilt Guild

La Jolla FiberArts Gallery

Margrette Carr

The fiber artist of today owes much to the many wonderful people and companies that provided the tools and materials used to create the works of art presented in this exhibit. Without the efforts of fabric manufacturers, quilt shops, guilds, artists, galleries and collectors, fiber art as we know and enjoy it would not be possible. Quilt Visions acknowledges and commends our valued sponsors for their many contributions to the arts.

Awards

The **Quilts Japan Prize,** sponsored by Nihon Vogue, a Japanese corporation, and awarded in 1994, 1996, 1998, and 2002, will once again be awarded to a **QUILT VISIONS 2004** artist. At the conclusion of this year's jurying process, the jurors selected Emily Richardson, of Philadelphia, Pennsylvania, to receive this award for her work *Before a Gate*. The objective of the Quilts Japan Prize is to express gratitude for the continued growth of the Japanese quilt, which is due in great part to American quilters, and to pay respect to the predecessors of quiltmaking. With this award, Nihon Vogue hopes to play a role in the development of quiltmaking by helping to link the ties between Japanese and American quiltmakers.

The **Sponsor's Award** is given by Rosie Gonzales of Rosie's Calico Cupboard Quilt Shop who selected Sachiko Sasakura, of Tokyo, Japan for her quilt *Another Member of My Family*. "The simplicity and detail of this wall hanging appealed to me immediately," said Rosie. "I loved the black and white concept. This cat just walks into my heart. If this were a photo of a cat that needed a home, I would have taken him in a minute. The artist captured the cat's expressions so well."

The **La Jolla FiberArts Award** is given by owner Lynn Noble, of La Jolla FiberArts Gallery. Nancy Crasco of Brighton, Massachusetts is the first recipient of this award for her work *Tunic of Tossing Leaves*. Lynn said of the work, "The piece perfectly represents contemporary quilt art, with the interesting departure towards the 'idea' of a wearable piece. Nancy has incorporated air, light, and a sense of ephemeral nature. One can only imagine the dreamy awareness of wearing such a piece." The award is an acknowledgement for artistic ability, and is intended to encourage fiber artists to explore more fully the medium of the art quilt.

The **CREAM Award** (Cathy Rasmussen Emerging Artist Memorial Award), is awarded by The Studio Art Quilt Association, a non-profit national organization founded to serve artists working in the quilt medium and presented to an artist with a work in a VISIONS exhibition for the first time. The CREAM Award is so named in memory of SAQA's first executive director, Cathy Rasmussen. The board of directors of SAQA has chosen Lori Lupe Pelish, of Niskayuna, New York, as the recipient of this year's award for her work *Bad News*.

The **Brakensiek "Caught Our Eye" Award** is presented to Ree Nancarrow of Denali Park, Alaska for her piece *Nenana Flats*. Nancy and Warren Brakensiek are longtime contemporary art quilt collectors living in Los Angeles. Their collection consists of over 140 art quilts. They believe that a collector's eye can be different from that of professional judges or experts.

The **President's Choice Award**, given by Canyon Quilters of San Diego, a non-profit organization established in 1985 to meet the needs of local quiltmakers in San Diego County, is chosen by the President of Quilt San Diego/Quilt Visions. Patti Sevier has selected *Porous Square* by Charlotte Bird.
"The visual impact of this piece draws the viewer in on many levels," said Patti.

Eva Aagesen
Flatsåvei
Norway

Light plays an important role in this transparent quilt.
As the light changes, the viewer may dimly see shades
of shapes which are fused to the back of the quilt. This
is a parallel to my source of inspiration: semi-
transparent ice flakes through which one dimly could
see the water slowly moving underneath.

I was fascinated by a view over the Baltic Sea on a cold
February morning when the rays of sunshine were
reflected on water and from ice; a peaceful, quiet view
by which my thoughts and mind were calmed. I wanted
to capture both this scenery and this state of mind and
depict it through my quilt. Transparent materials, metal
organza and shiny, small beads underline this
impression of clear, cold, fresh and refreshing air.

Appliqué
Hand embellished
Machine embellished
Machine quilted

Deidre Adams

Littleton, Colorado
USA

This quilt is part of a series exploring the use of abstract imagery to create impressions that are seasonal yet timeless, based on elements of nature, but filtered through a complex web of partially formed thoughts or memories. *Nocturne* uses a dark color scheme. To some it might be a kind of landscape; to others it might suggest the idea of water, perhaps seen at night. I leave it to the viewer to decide.

I love creating a rich texture with machine quilting, and I also love to paint. I'm exploring techniques for combining these two favorite media using the quilt as a canvas.

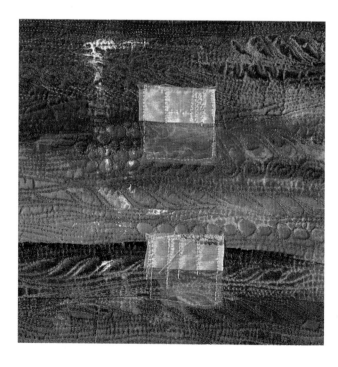

Machine pieced
Appliqué
Machine quilted
Hand painted

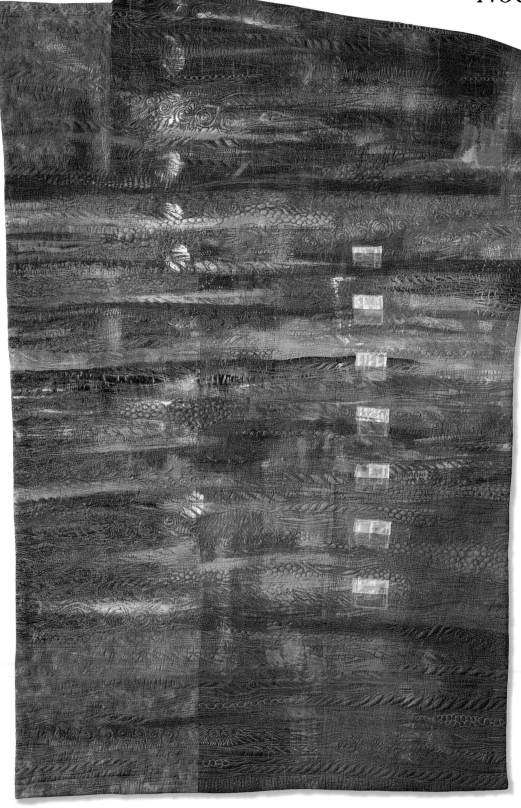

Bettina Andersen

Copenhagen
Denmark

In this series of quilts I am trying to quilt with fabrics and threads like a painter with paint. I have chosen quilting and not painting because quilting adds textures to my works which are not possible in painting. This specific quilt symbolizes melancholy. It is an attempt to visualize melancholy.

Machine pieced
Appliqué
Hand embellished
Machine quilted

*Melancholy
(Abstract Paintings VI)*
40″ x 50″

Rebecca Barr

San Marcos, California
USA

A strong emotional reaction to something, a place or an experience, creates an indelible memory. This quilt was inspired by memories of a dramatic coastline, whose spectacular appearance compelled in me a powerful personal response. We are drawn to such places by their beauty and mystery. What is seen on the surface is shaped by what lies beneath and one's experience of the place is formed by its wildness: by the uncontrollable rhythms and forces of nature.

This piece was constructed from a single piece of fabric hand-dyed by Judy Robertson. By appliquéing parts of the piece in other locations I was able to create movement and depth in the composition by emphasizing a flowing connectedness among the design elements and by accepting the ambiguous relationship between the negative and positive spaces.

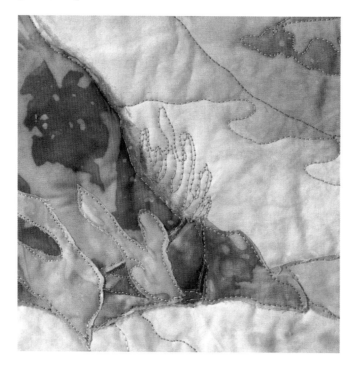

Appliqué
Machine quilted

16

Seaswept

33″ x 36″

Charlotte Bird

San Diego, California
USA

Annie Dillard writes of a fellow sitting in a cabin teaching a stone to talk. The Incas taught stones to speak of perfecting shape and fit. In the American Southwest, stones express perfecting color by sunlight, chemistry, and time. I am exploring the perfect speech of stones in shapes. My stitches percolate among the stones, seeking their words. This piece is my current favorite of explorations completed and continuing. I thank Andy Goldsworthy for inspiring the first study.

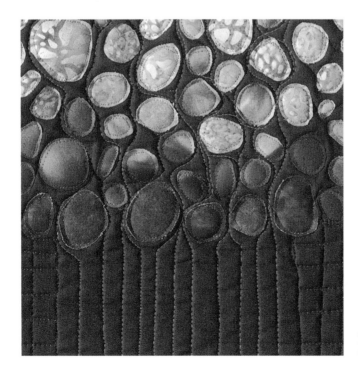

Appliqué
Machine quilted

Porous Squares

38″ x 37″
President's Choice Award

Marie Castle Wing

Mead, Colorado
USA

Weavings #12 is part of a continuing series that features numerous multicolored woven strips intertwined to create a sense of depth and mystery.

Originally conceived as small individual works, the blocks drew strength from each other. When the pieces begged to become one, who was I not to sew them together?

Machine pieced
Machine quilted
Fused appliqué

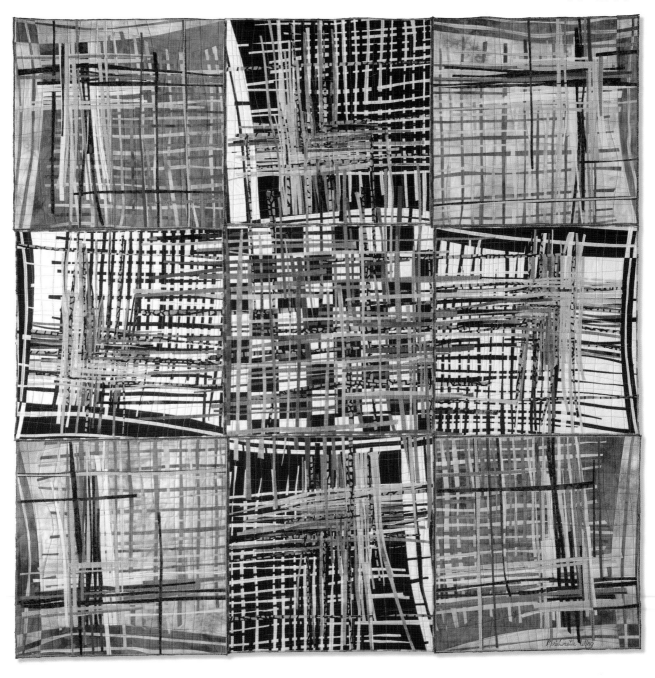

Jette Clover

Cocoa, Florida
USA

Upon discovering the extent to which tests and textbooks are being censored by bias and sensitivity committees, I wanted to express my concern about their redefining of reality and rewriting of literature. The committees subject all educational publishing to long lists of banned words, ideas, and topics. Every conceivable controversial subject gets deleted, every political and social issue excluded, and the language itself scrubbed to make it utterly inoffensive to all potential readers. The result is boring, inane text with no resemblance to the world we live in, and it is utterly disrespectful to all writers.

Machine pieced
Appliqué
Hand quilted
Machine quilted
Collage technique

 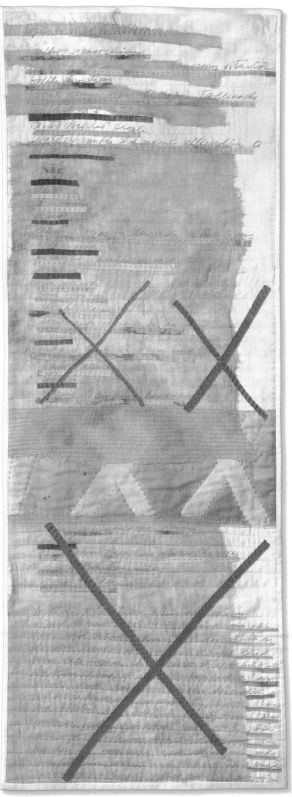

Nancy Cordry

Federal Way, Washington
USA

While on a visit to Arizona, I happened upon an old craggy giant Saguaro Cactus (*cereus giganteus*). As I studied it, I noticed all the holes, prickly parts, lines, wrinkles, rotting areas and colors, and did a few sketches. Once home, I began playing and puttering around with my fabric collection and ended up with a sense of that old cactus, but something different.

Machine pieced
Machine quilted

Cacti 1

50″ x 54″

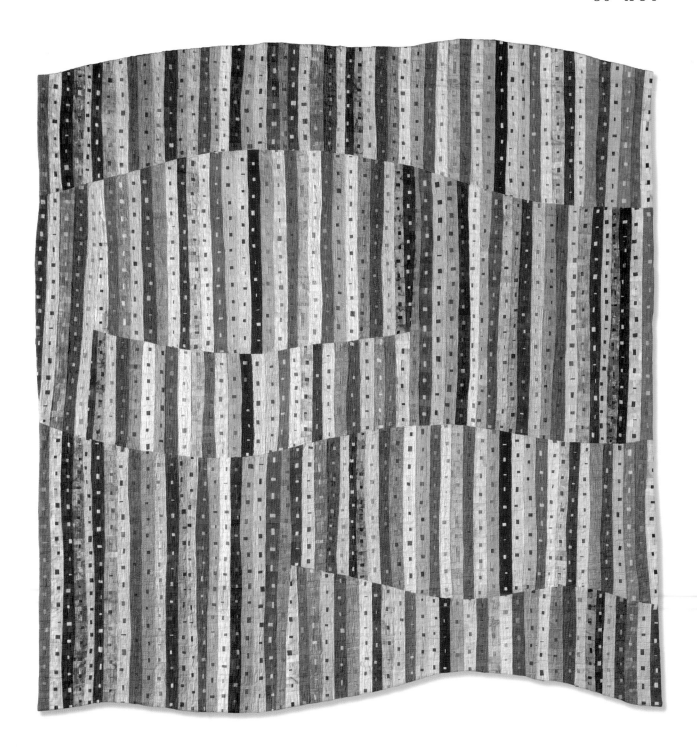

Nancy Crasco

Brighton, Massachusetts
USA

The design was inspired by a photograph of a Peruvian
woven tunic of the Wari Culture (600-850 AD).

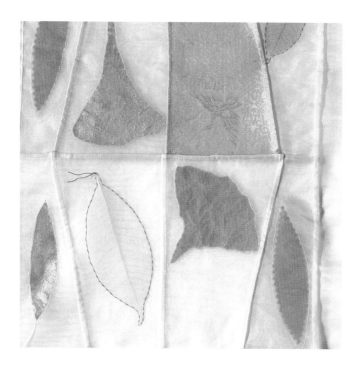

Machine pieced
Hand quilted

26

Tunic of Tossing Leaves

72″ x 38″

The La Jolla FiberArts Award

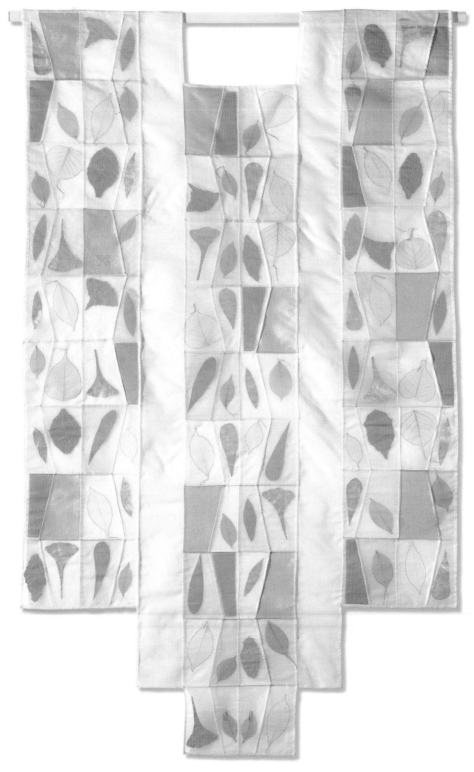

Helene Davis

Paducah, Kentucky
USA

This piece is dedicated to my dentist, Dr. Jon Bartlett, who sounds like a pear but is really a peach.

Machine pieced
Machine quilted

Tooth I: Root Canals

31″ x 27″

Malka Dubrawsky

Austin, Texas
USA

Kente was inspired by my love of batik, African fabric and the process of cutting and reassembling fabric. The starting points for this piece were two similarly-colored pieces of fabric that I had patterned to look plaid-like. One piece had started life as a solid black fabric, been resisted with wax, discharged, dyed, resisted a second time and redyed. The other grew in a similar fashion but began its journey as white fabric. Both were lovely pieces as yardage, but when I cut them up and sewed them back together, they wove into an image that was greater than the sum of its parts.

Machine pieced
Hand embellished
Hand quilted

Jane Einhorn

Albuquerque, New Mexico
USA

This quilt is a celebration of the monumental earnestness that goes into the deep commitment to find ways to celebrate diversity. Despite the tremendous difficulty of creating room for differences, for developing joy in one another and peace among us – we continue to fight for and know that the celebration of diversity is good for all of us. As a fat, middle-aged, Jewish lesbian psychotherapist, I have often had the role of bridge, to connect individuals or some group with an uncomfortably different other. I have found in earnestness the shared blessing of being human – that while we seldom know the right answer to the most important and complex of questions, I honor the many of us who with dedication and perseverance march toward what we believe.

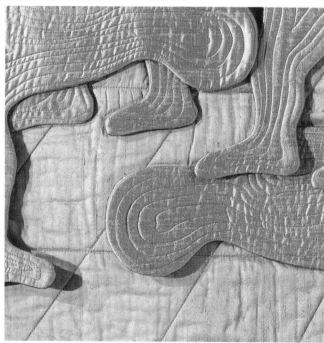

Machine pieced
Machine quilted
Hand constructed

Sometimes We Are More Earnest Than Wise

40″ x 64″

Noriko Endo

Narashino
Japan

When I visited Oregon, I was fascinated by the beauty of
tall trees, the verdant sweeps of woods and the various
shades of green. The wet mosses on the tree trunks had
drawn me to my art. The changing light, reflection and
color always excite me.

Appliqué
Machine embellished
Machine quilted

Nature in Oregon
62″ x 88″

Pamela Fitzsimons

Mount Vincent, New South Wales
Australia

The ancient Australian landscape, shaped by the elements and marked by time, is a constant source of inspiration. Time passed is recorded in the Permian fossils exposed in layers in the uplifted sandstone walls of Bow Wow Gorge.

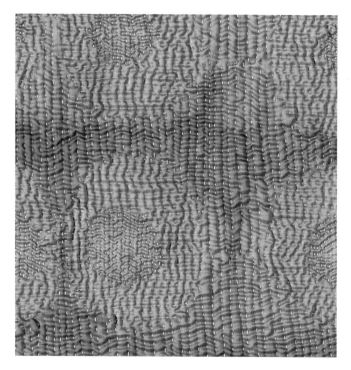

Machine pieced
Hand quilted
Hand dyed with eucalyptus
leaves

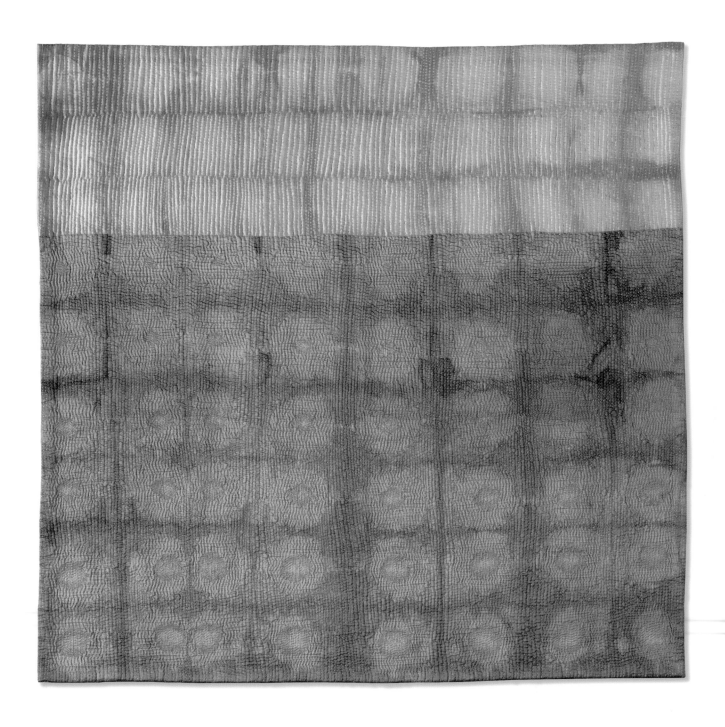

Ruth Garrison

Flagstaff, Arizona
USA

In all of the quilts in my Net series, I have presented simple, stable, calm compositions. At the same time, I have tried to hold the interest of the viewer with variation in color, value, and form.

Machine pieced
Machine quilted

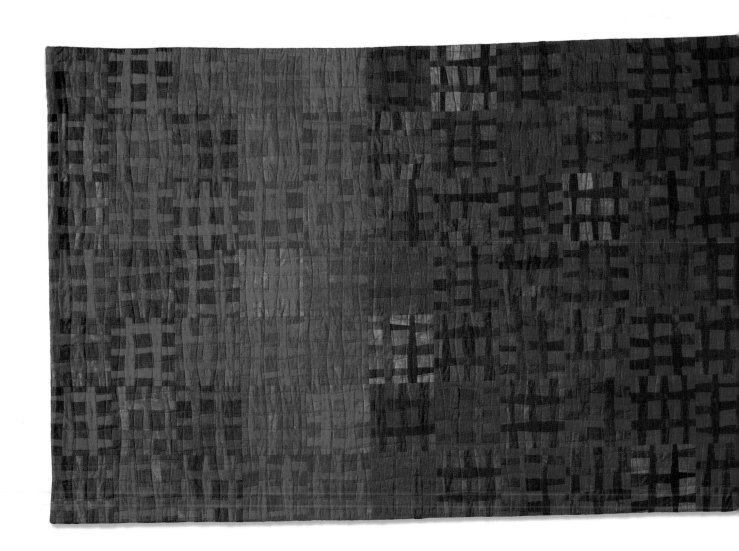

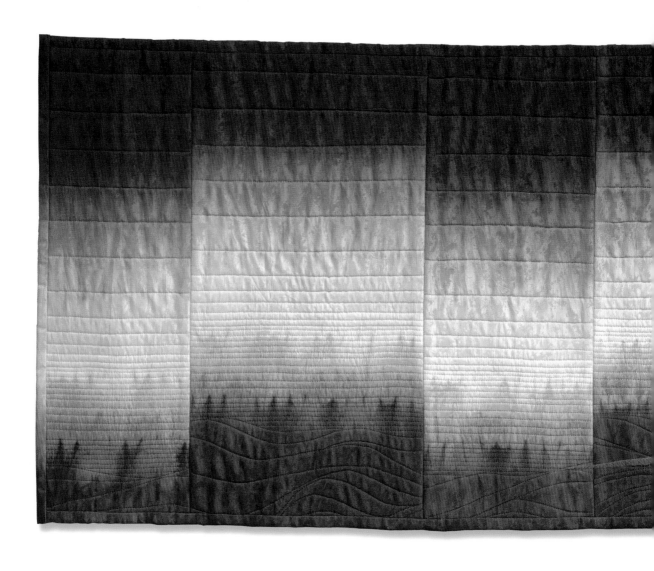

Leesa Zarinelli Gawlik
La Maddalena, Italy
Hometown: Ste. Genevieve, Missouri, USA

Northern Light was inspired by a journey on the eve of the millennium – December 31, 1999.
Flying from America to our home in Japan, the airline traveled over the rugged wilderness of
Alaska. Witnessing the endless range of mountains below was an experience never to be
forgotten. As we flew west, the setting sun began to illuminate the mountain tops. Suddenly,
a dagger of color stretched across the range, piercing it with fiery brilliance. Just as quickly,
the beauty of the image vanished with the sun. It is forever imprinted on my memory and
serves as a reminder to appreciate the glory that surrounds us, however fleeting it may be.

Northern Light

14″ x 54″

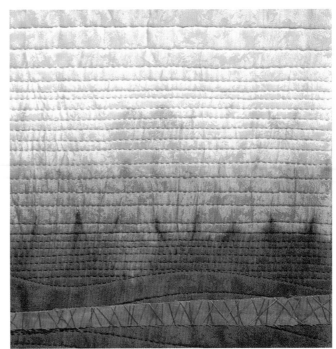

Machine pieced
Hand embellished
Machine quilted
Shibori dyed with indigo, onion skin,
green tea, wood chips

Bean Gilsdorf

Portland, Oregon
USA

This quilt is part of an ongoing series that examines violence and loss.

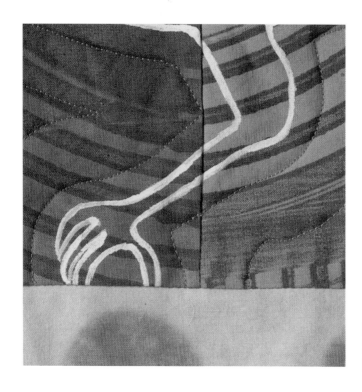

Machine pieced
Machine quilted
Machine appliqué

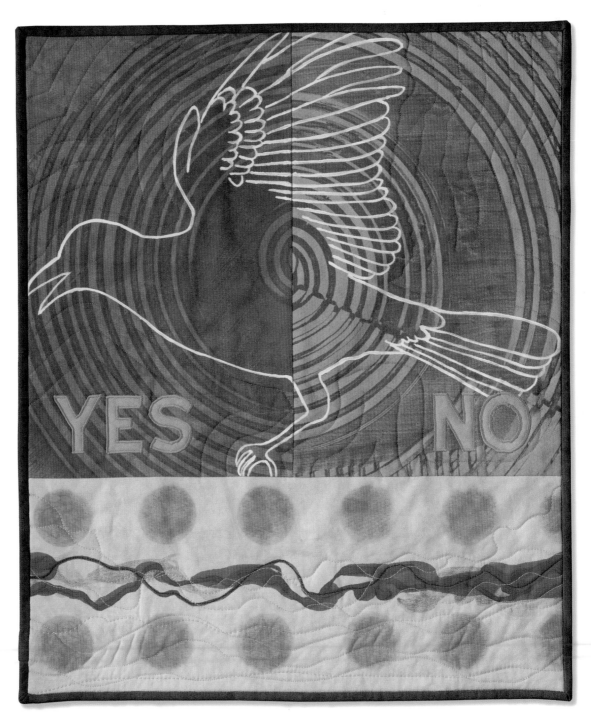

Margery Goodall

Mount Lawley, Western Australia
Australia

This quilt is one in a series about perceptions and associations. The design relates to aspects of the Australian landscape.

I enjoy working with line, both in quilts and other art media. In quilts, I currently work with line in a number of styles. This particular style was inspired by patterning, observed both in nature and in the work of hand weavers.

Machine pieced
Machine quilted

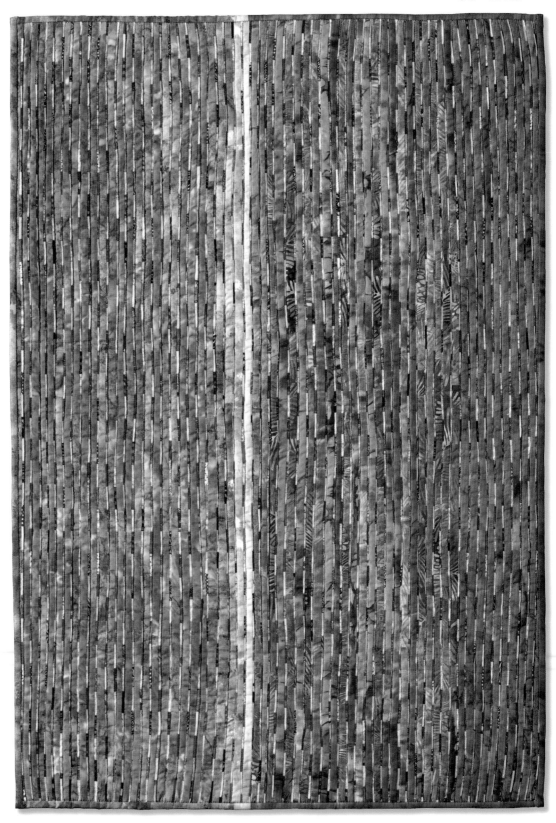

Mi Sik Kim

Seoul
South Korea

We are living surrounded by many kinds of walls, visible or invisible. When looking at the wall, sometimes it gives me warm and comfortable feelings. Sometimes I even feel that the wall is talking to me. I tried to express these feelings in my work *The Wall*.

Machine pieced
Appliqué
Hand quilted

Eileen Lauterborn

Farmingdale, New York
USA

This work is an exploration of how lines can build into forms while creating their own linear rhythms. The texture of the background surface and the colored forms beneath the lines are intended to add dimension to the composition.

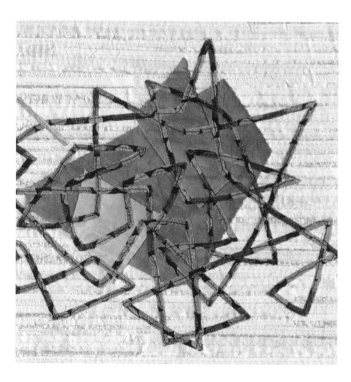

Appliqué
Machine embellished
Machine quilted

Wendy Lugg

Bull Creek, Western Australia
Australia

Born into an Australian family heritage of thrift and making
do, I grew up understanding that with a little imagination
and makeshift materials, it was possible to create wonders.
The same heritage of ingenuity born of necessity is evident
in my ever growing collection of old Japanese fabrics.

I feel a strong affinity to these carefully mended fragments,
bearing patched holes and faded areas which provide
tantalizing glimpses into their past. Some of my old
fragments demand to be left as they are. Others beg to be
recycled into new works which honor their heritage, and
mine.

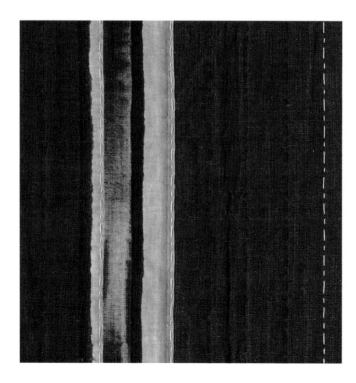

Hand pieced
Machine pieced
Hand quilted

Linda MacDonald

Willits, California
USA

In California, our scenic wild lands (private and public) are being converted into vineyards, recreational housing, suburbs, and commercial development. As these areas become scarcer, decisions will have to be made on the value of these wild lands. Is it important for us to sustain (with our tax dollars) undeveloped land as habitats for wildlife and as sanctuaries for us? I feel we do not want to wait until there is not much left to save to make these decisions.

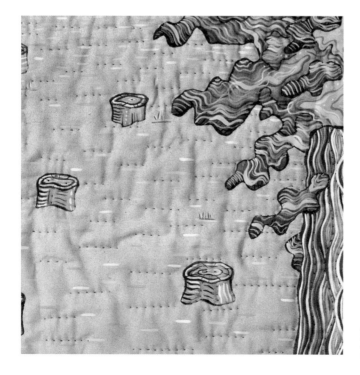

Hand quilted
Painted

Inge Mardal & Steen Hougs

Chantilly
France

This quilt is inspired by a lovely and sumptuous flower turning a ditch into a small paradise, where we at twilight time met these two butterflies, who enjoyed a sweet meal and apparently also the company of each other.

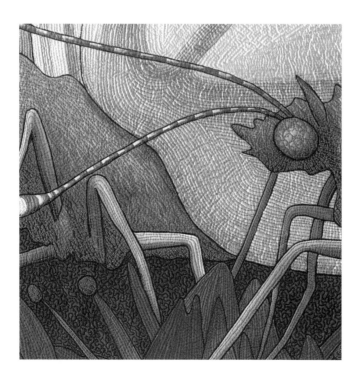

Machine quilted
Hand painted

Barbara McKie

Lyme, Connecticut
USA

Flowers, particularly lilies, have inspired many of my pieces. This water lily was photographed on a long vacation trip in 2002 from Connecticut to Colorado. I painted the background leaves and water on silk and used disperse dye to print the image of the flower on polyester crepe. The polymer clay work I do went into the eyes of the dragonfly.

Machine appliqué
Machine embellished
Machine quilted

Patricia Mink

Johnson City, Tennessee
USA

Layers are the focus of my work in several ways:

- as complex metaphor

- as components of physical and visual structure

- as elements of process

For me, layers echo the processes of learning and understanding, while also evoking a sense of time. Repeated patterns and imagery in my work function as personal iconography. Their meanings can be very specific, but are also intended to speak on a more general or universal level, addressing issues of individual development and shared human experience.

My work is primarily textile based, and for me has strong connections to the history of that medium and its contextual associations. At the same time, I enjoy pushing the boundaries of traditional forms through the use of non-traditional materials and techniques.

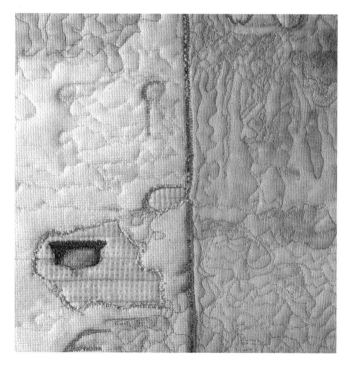

Machine embellished
Hand quilted
Machine quilted
Fused appliqué

Ree Nancarrow

Denali Park, Alaska
USA

The Pratt Museum in Homer, Alaska invited me to participate in a multi-media show called "Wetlands: Going With the Flow." My studio and living room windows look across a small glacial lake which is a beautiful little pocket of wetlands. An integral part of my life for 39 years has been to watch the daily, seasonal and yearly changes of that view and its inhabitants.

However, the wetlands are truly different and expansive in Nenana, which I drive through on my way to town. The black spruce decorate the horizon with their unique narrow silhouettes and sparse branches. A lower elevation allows different species to live there, among them the iris and the cattails.

Machine pieced
Machine quilted
Hand-dyed
Hand painted and silk screened images

Nenana Flats
46″ x 48″

Brakensiek "Caught Our Eye" Award

Miriam Nathan-Roberts

Berkeley, California
USA

In February 2001, I tripped and shattered my wrist. Two surgeries followed, including a bone graft, a metal plate, and an "external fixator" (a metal apparatus with bars going into the bone).

I was told that it was impossible to predict, for the first year, how much of my hand function would return. A major part of my life was threatened: quilting, dyeing, and printing. This piece celebrates my regaining full use of my hand.

The central panel is layered images. Its background is the interior of the bone enlarged. A wooden mannequin hand, and a medical illustration of the bones of the hand, are superimposed. A photograph of my arm wearing the "external fixator" is uppermost.

The border is all hand printed, hand dyed, or hand discharged fabric (except for one commercial print): the majority by the artist. The diamonds refer to the tradition of quilting, and they are layered with tracings of my hand.

Machine pieced
Appliqué
Machine quilted
Hand dyed and painted fabric
Digitally printed fabric

Brenda Norquay

Orkney Islands
Scotland, United Kingdom

Recently Britain suffered the largest epidemic of foot and mouth disease in the world, caused by contaminated meat from another country which resulted in the slaughter of over four million animals on 9,627 farms. As a significant event in agriculture, this tragedy should be commemorated and should act as a reminder to politicians to implement tougher controls on illegal meat imports which pose a disease threat, as it resulted in our farmers having to make "a devastating journey from darkness to light."

Repeated boxes of contrasting imagery imply motion (i.e., the passage of time), and each strives to evoke a mood, memory, sound, or experience of the event by means of materials, technique and content, using the interplay of transparent quilt layers, together with the varied spacing, length, or texture of stitched threads to convey feeling and concepts.

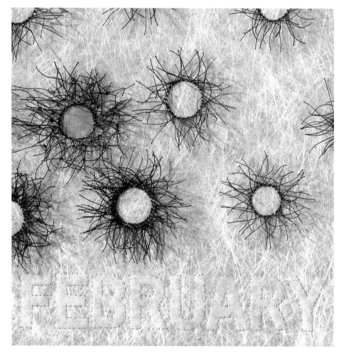

Hand embellished
Hand quilted
Hand tied quilting ('knots' are a common link used in farming and quiltmaking)
Shadow quilted text
Transfer printed images

Mitsue Ohno

Sanbu-gun, Chiba
Japan

The design of this quilt consists of three parts. The main color of the left part of this quilt is yellow-green, representing the season of new green leaves. Images of "a fun summer festival" are portrayed in the center, and "spinning pin wheels" are shown in the right. The top and bottom borders of the quilt came from the neckline of the kimono. The kimono has a pattern of cherry blossoms all over. My mother made this kimono for me when I was 18 years old. Since this is my precious kimono, I unstitched it and used it for my quilt instead of cutting it with scissors.

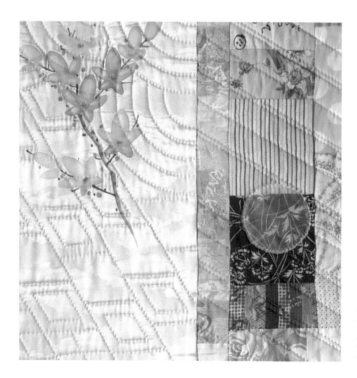

Hand pieced
Appliqué
Hand quilted

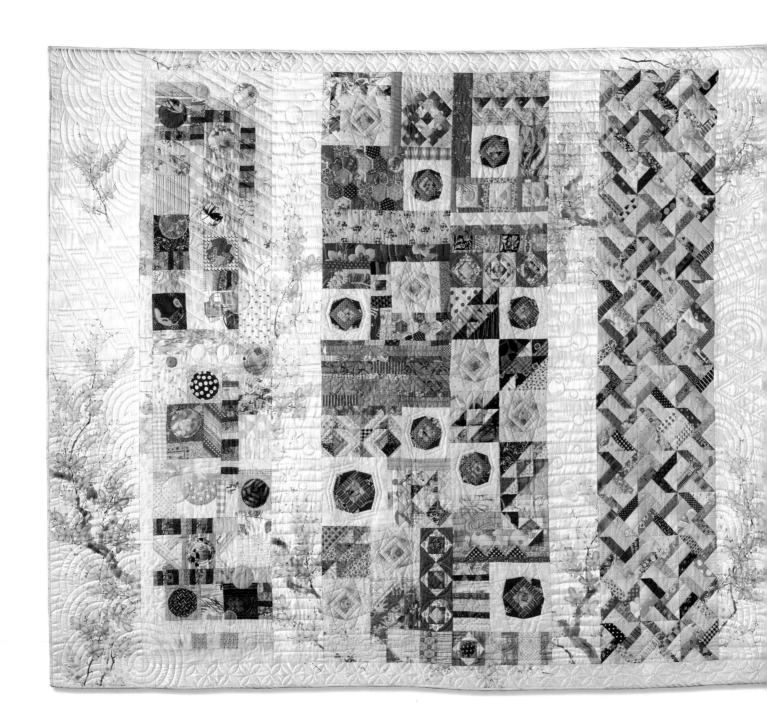

Dan Olfe

Julian, California
USA

I have long been fascinated by the beautiful color images that appear in water reflections. This quilt is part of a series in which I use 3-D software to reflect different patterns in simulated water surfaces. For this quilt I started with a grid of vertical blue and green lines, which were crossed at intervals by horizontal yellow, orange, and red lines. The reflected image represents the topography of the water waves. The computer image was printed on polyester cloth by a dye-sublimation process.

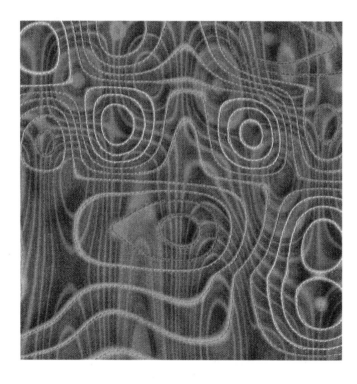

Machine quilted
Dye sublimation print

Wave Topography

36″ x 24″

Lori Lupe Pelish

Niskayuna, New York
USA

Unsettling amounts of bad news overwhelm a family as they try to cope with their sorrow, anger and grief.

Appliqué
Machine embellished
Machine quilted

Clare Plug
Napier
New Zealand

I made this quilt as a tribute to one of my favorite New Zealand artists, Ralph Hotere. He is masterful in his ability to create wonderful illusions and his understanding of the huge range of possibilities of the color 'black.' I admire too how he is able to create his powerful artworks from the most unlikely materials.

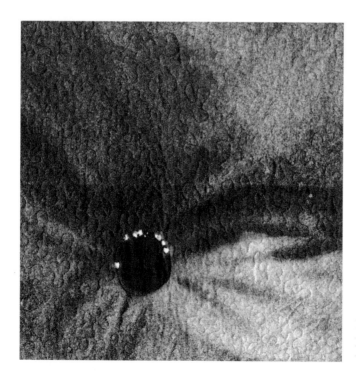

Machine pieced
Machine quilted
Discharge-dyed cotton

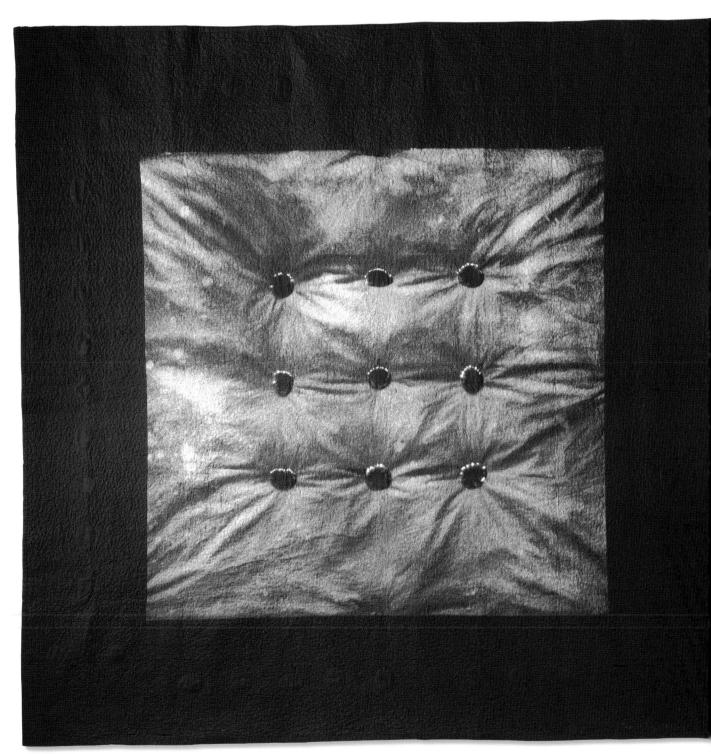

Toot Reid

Tacoma, Washington
USA

We are all an assemblage of pieces: pieces of memories, of emotions, of relationships, of experiences. We collect and catalog the pieces and tuck them away, to be consciously and unconsciously dug up later, hoping to find ourselves. I am endlessly arranging and rearranging the pieces. My work is an exploration of this process, its uncertainties, randomness, indefinable nature, and its endless manifestations.

Machine pieced
Appliqué
Hand quilted

Emily Richardson

Philadelphia, Pennsylvania
USA

Images of gates depict a range of symbols and metaphors, but generally they represent either a barrier or a passage from one place, condition, or state of mind to another. Here the gate represents my transition from the physical world to the worlds of spirit and imagination. Standing before this gate I reflect on what brings me to this point and to what possibilities might exist on the other side. The prospect is inviting; the gate is not always open.

Hand appliqué
Hand quilted
Silk fabric
Acrylic paint

Before a Gate

65″ x 34″
Quilts Japan Prize

Noël Ruessmann

Stroudsburg, Pennsylvania
USA

Once, over 20 years ago, I saw a few Himalayan blue poppies blooming in the Royal Botanic Garden, Edinburgh. The sight was celestial. Here, I imagined a monochromatic, schematic field of the poppies in bloom. The rhythmic pattern of the quilting suggests the waving movement of budding stalks and grasses in the wind, broad swaths from a large paint brush (such as I used to paint the flowers), and a dry Zen garden's raked gravel.

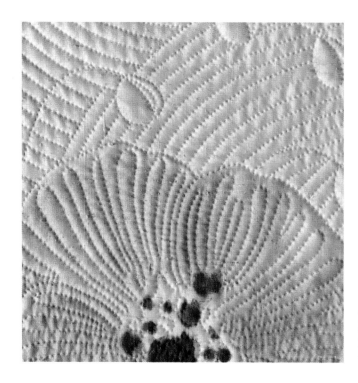

Machine pieced
Hand quilted
Painted surface design

Blue Poppies
42″ x 67″

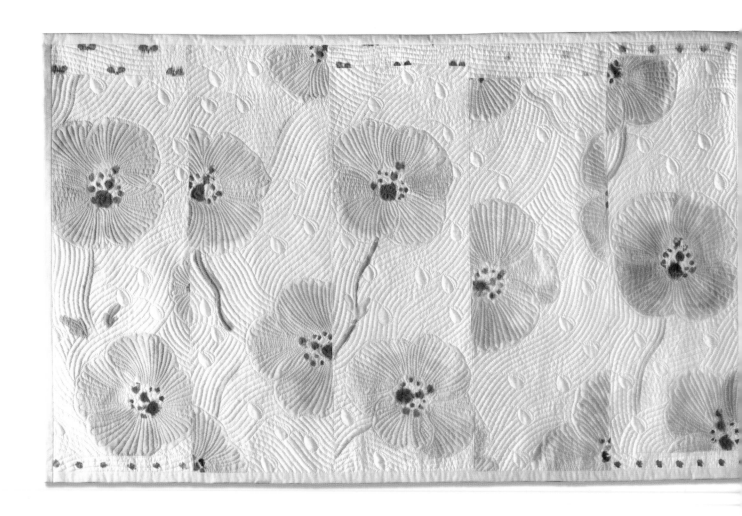

Sachiko Sasakura

Tokyo
Japan

I have been working on my quilts featuring Genki (cheer), the little cat my daughter found on the street. Genki, who was 17cm in length and weighed only 250 g seven years ago, now weighs more than 4kg and surely is a big member of my family. On top of offering me the ideas of making quilts, she gives us cheer and casual topics of conversation.

Machine pieced
Appliqué
Machine quilted

Another Member of My Family #11

72″ x 84″

Sponsor's Award

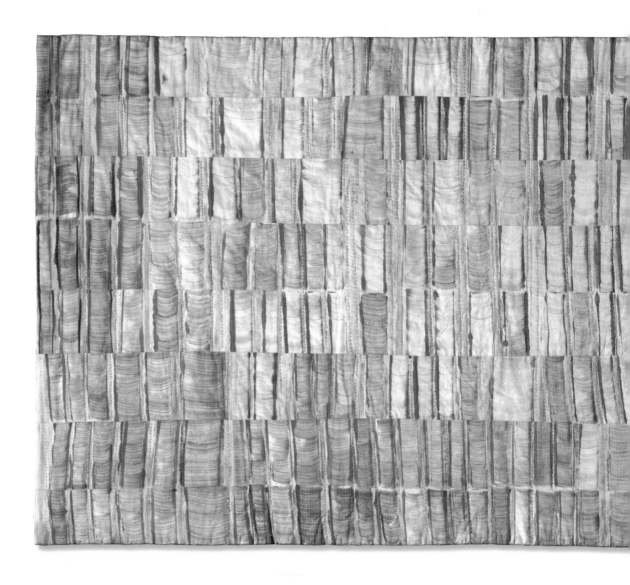

Connie Scheele

Houston, Texas
USA

A love of the lakes and woods of northern Wisconsin has
been the inspiration for my work for the past 10 years. This
piece, and its two predecessors, came from the connection
to that environment and my exploration of mono-printing. If
the work relates a feeling of looking through the woods by
using a straightforward, linear image, then I have achieved
my goal.

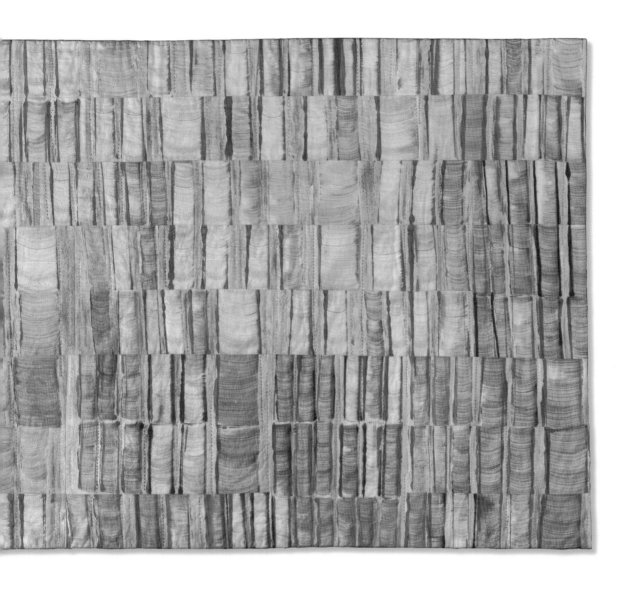

Through the Woods

37″ x 85″

Machine pieced
Hand quilted
Hand monoprinted

Patti Shaw

Seattle, Washington
USA

The image on this quilt is from a photo I took of an old wooden santo from the Philippines. Originally the figure would have been beautifully dressed and displayed in a church, village chapel, or family devotional shrine. The worn, vulnerable look and the mystery that surrounds her is what inspired me to create this piece.

Hand embellished
Hand quilted
Photo transferred
Painted

Santa Maria

44″ x 24″

Susan Shie

Wooster, Ohio
USA

I have a pair of beautiful blue leather pumps with several colors of leather flower and leaf appliqués — and then there are these cute little red heels. Very sweet. They don't even fit, but I bought them at Goodwill, just for the art they really are.

My artists' support group chose shoes as our theme for this year's show. I decided I needed to put these shoes into a quilt, so I stuck them on St. Quilta's feet, and I made her flipping pancakes in the kitchen.

When I got done airbrushing the composition, I decided this St. Q. is really Jimmy in drag, because she's so muscular and is flipping those flapjacks in the iron skillet so easily! I'm just watching in sheer admiration.

I saved almost all the diary writing for when I was quilting the piece, adding new adventure stories as I worked. I think most of the stories are about the terrible snowy weather of that winter. Yikes! But the kitchen was always warm.

Hand embellished
Hand quilted
Airbrush painted

Wendy Slotboom

Seattle, Washington
USA

I used a very controlled, contained technique to create a
quilt that, I hope, strikes the viewer as being exuberant
and joyful.

A simple "X" shape becomes imbued with personality as it
steps "outside the box."

Machine pieced
Machine quilted

Carol Taylor

Pittsford, New York
USA

Intertwined refers to the illusion of a woven pattern, but also the intermingling of past and up-to-the-minute influences, as a return to the basic block and structural grid of traditional quilts combines with the innovation of improvisational curved piecing and decorative stitching.

The plays of color and value in blocks and striped patterns serve to elongate some blocks, shake up any regularity, and energize the field. Patterns of broad and narrow linear elements encourage the viewer to perceive an over and under illusion, a sensed intertwining of layers. This piece was created using hand dyed cottons and a single commercial striped fabric.

A free motion "connection stitch" in rayon threads echoes the blocks and lines, and also mimics the miniaturized technology that helps us interconnect to create the social fabric of our lives.

Machine pieced
Machine quilted

Kristin Tweed

North Fort Myers, Florida
USA

I hope to reveal the character of the model. I use a gesture drawing as the basis for my quilts. Interesting distortions occur. Somehow the distortions define the person more clearly than a straight forward record of their features. A secondary stitched portrait is at right angles to the primary image. The secondary portrait symbolizes lives not lived, careers not followed, lovers not married, children not born. What if.....

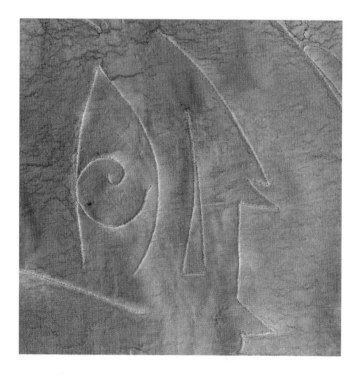

Machine quilted
Hand painted

#15 Big Head Series - The Kimono

38″ x 38″

Melitta VanderBrooke

Newtown, Pennsylvania
USA

This quilt was created as a memorial to my
mother, who passed away last May. It's a tribute
to her strength and courage and represents all
those things that remain unsaid.

Machine pieced
Machine quilted
Hand painted fabrics

Nelda Warkentin

Anchorage, Alaska
USA

My abstract painted silk compositions are unique, colorful, beautiful, and refined. I work primarily in pattern using designs that are simple, but interesting. My work expresses perfection and restraint.

I use line, pattern and color together to express movement, a memory, mood, or idea. The inspiration for my work comes largely from nature.

Autumn Splendor illustrates the colors and shapes of autumn – the leaves, birch bark, sky, sunset, etc. One day while looking out my window, a woman walking up the street with a purple umbrella caught my attention. At that moment, the color of the autumn leaves and sky was breathtaking. Over the next few weeks, I kept thinking about what I had seen. The result is *Autumn Splendor*.

Machine pieced
Machine quilted
Multiple layers of acrylic painted silk over acrylic painted canvas

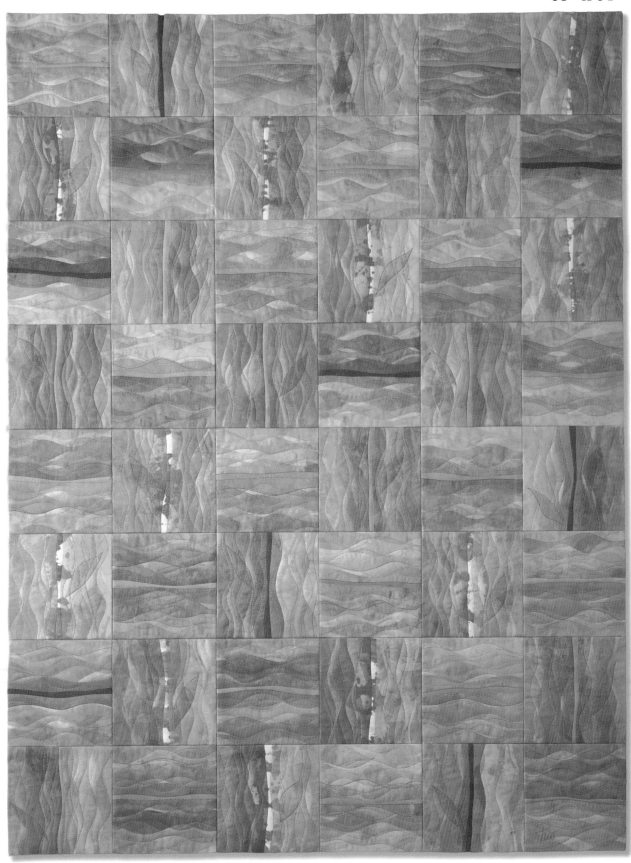

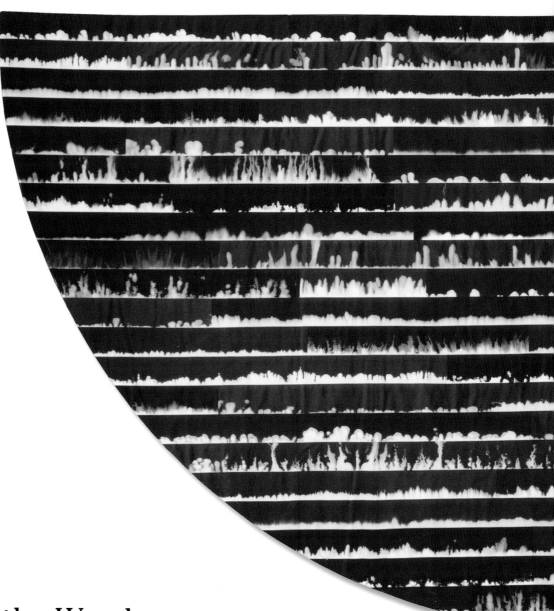

Martha Warshaw

Cincinnati, Ohio
USA

This quilt came about after visits to several museums where vestments marked by centuries of use were on display. Also evident in this quilt is the impression made by studying the work of Agnes Martin.

Cope: Burning

53″ x 106″

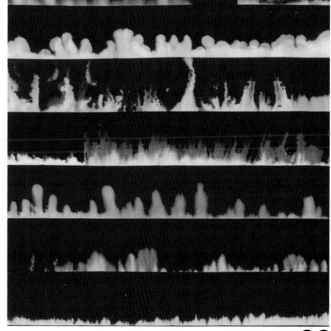

Machine pieced
Hand quilted
Discharge dye

Artists & Quilts Index

Aagesen, Eva	*Frost*	10
Adams, Deidre	*Nocturne*	12
Andersen, Bettina	*Melancholy (Abstract Paintings VI)*	14
Barr, Rebecca	*Seaswept*	16
Bird, Charlotte	*Porous Square*	18
Castle Wing, Marie	*Weavings #12*	20
Clover, Jette	*The Language Police*	22
Cordry, Nancy	*Cacti 1*	24
Crasco, Nancy	*Tunic of Tossing Leaves*	26
Davis, Helene	*Tooth I: Root Canals*	28
Dubrawsky, Malka	*Kente*	30
Einhorn, Jane	*Sometimes We Are More Earnest Than Wise*	32
Endo, Noriko	*Nature in Oregon*	34
Fitzsimons, Pamela	*Fossil Bed #3*	36
Garrison, Ruth	*Net 4*	38
Gawlik, Leesa Zarinelli	*Northern Light*	40
Gilsdorf, Bean	*Frequency*	42
Goodall, Margery	*Iceline (Weave #4)*	44
Kim, Mi Sik	*The Wall*	46
Lauterborn, Eileen	*Between the Lines*	48
Lugg, Wendy	*Faded Memories V*	50
MacDonald, Linda	*Tree Park*	52
Mardal, Inge & Hougs, Steen	*Twilight Rendezvous*	54
McKie, Barbara	*Water Ballet #5*	56
Mink, Patricia	*Tapia #5*	58
Nancarrow, Ree	*Nenana Flats*	60
Nathan-Roberts, Miriam	*Fracture*	62
Norquay, Brenda	*Journey*	64
Ohno, Mitsue	*Dream Quilt*	66
Olfe, Dan	*Wave Topography*	68
Pelish, Lori Lupe	*Bad News*	70
Plug, Clare	*To R.H.*	72
Reid, Toot	*Thirteen*	74
Richardson, Emily	*Before a Gate*	76
Ruessmann, Noel	*Blue Poppies*	78
Sasakura, Sachiko	*Another Member of My Family #11*	80
Scheele, Connie	*Through the Woods*	82
Shaw, Patti	*Santa Maria*	84
Shie, Susan	*St. Q's Kitchen Shoes*	86
Slotboom, Wendy	*Stepping Out*	88
Taylor, Carol	*Intertwined*	90
Tweed, Kristin	*#15 Big Head Series - The Kimono*	92
VanderBrooke, Melitta	*Memorial*	94
Warkentin, Nelda	*Autumn Splendor*	96
Warshaw, Martha	*Cope: Burning*	98